ISBN 978-0-578-13426-0

When My Hero Left

by Paul Singleton

Printed by CreateSpace, An Amazon.com Company

for Grant, Paige, Kelly, and Clark

drinking
gourd
press

I used to think that my Daddy was the strongest man in the whole world. He would toss me up in the air and then catch me before I fell.

It made my heart skip a beat, but I liked that game.

Whenever we played basketball with our neighbors, I swear I saw my Daddy fly.

Wherever we went, Daddy had a way of telling a story that made everybody want to laugh out loud!

When I was little, I used to think my Daddy knew all the answers.

If he didn't know the answer, he would try to figure it out.

He was my hero. And I wanted to be just like him! Just like My Daddy.

I listened to what he said and I paid attention to how he treated people. He was never too busy to help a person in need.

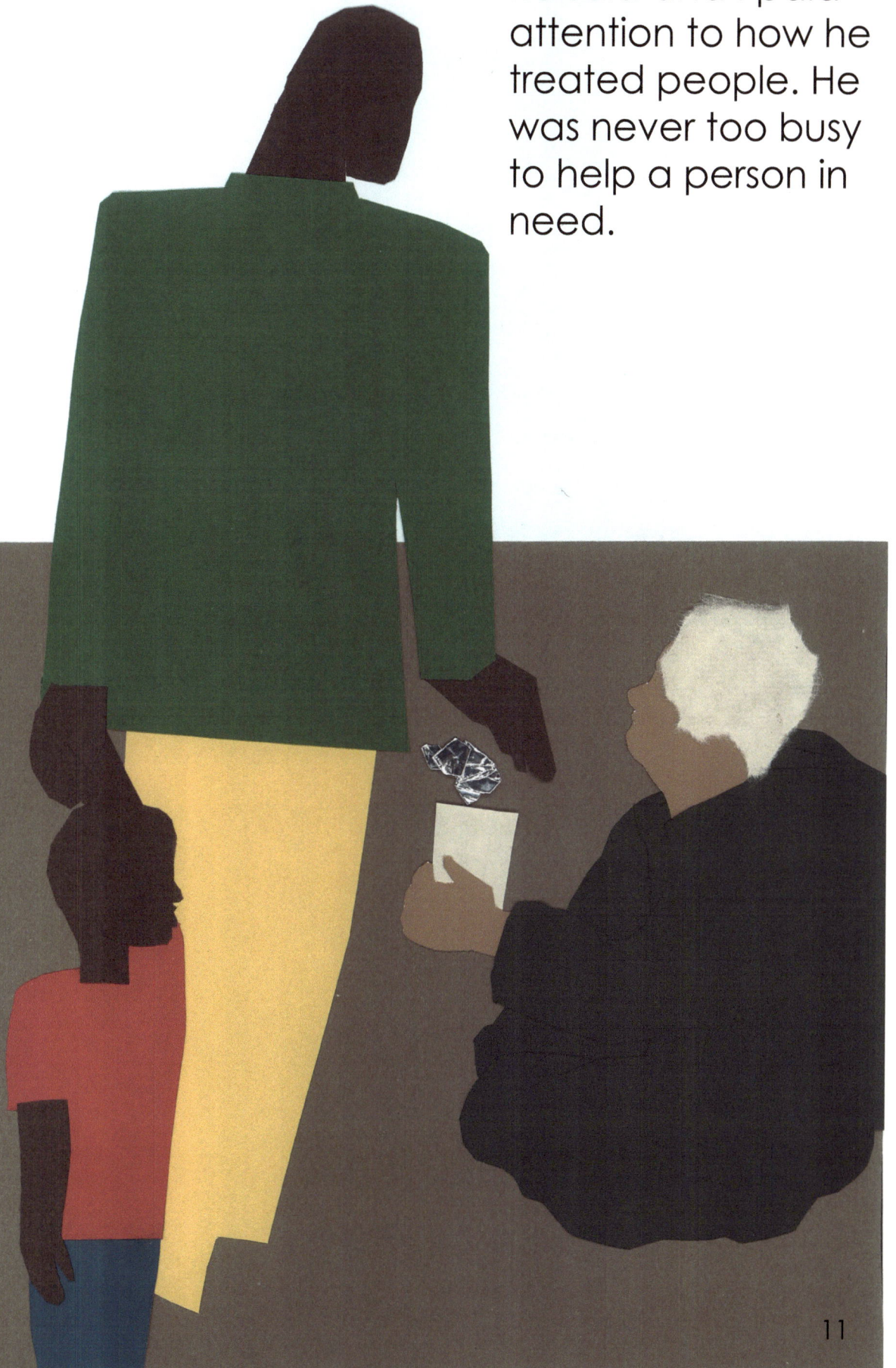

Then one day Daddy started having pains in his body.

Soon he didn't have that much energy. Doing normal things made him tired. He would have to stop and take a breath.

He walked like his legs were very heavy. He couldn't keep his eyes open. I couldn't tell if he was asleep or awake. But I knew that something was wrong.

13

Daddy had always helped other people, but now he was the one who needed help.

We went to the hospital a lot and saw a lot of doctors. They all tried to help Daddy get better, but I could see he wasn't getting any better.

Daddy didn't look so strong anymore- he just looked sick and felt tired all the time.

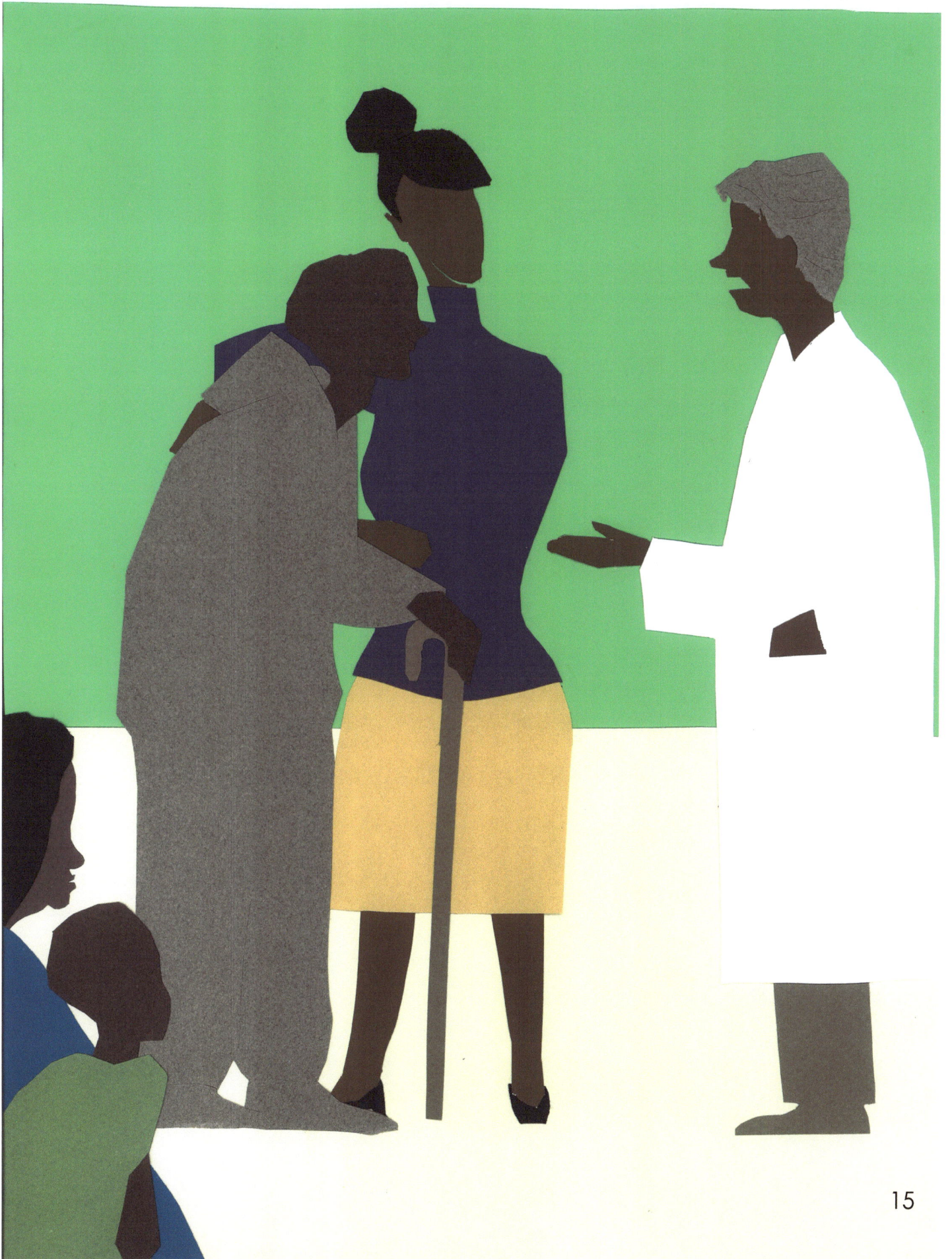

After a while Daddy went to stay in a place called a hospice, a special place for people who are dying. My Mama told me they were going to take good care of Daddy at the hospice.

My Daddy was dying and he was not coming back home.

When we visited I was too scared to say very much. I didn't like seeing my Daddy the way he looked in that bed. And I was scared. I didn't know what it means to "die".

At the funeral, everyone was dressed in all black. They looked down at the ground a lot and there was a lot of crying.

Our whole family was there, friends and neighbors too. Some of them stood up and talked about how special my Daddy was. Everybody had good memories of my Daddy.

All I could think about was how much I wanted him to come back.

After the funeral there was lots of food around, but I wasn't very hungry.

There was a picture of Daddy in a beautiful wreath of flowers. I couldn't stop staring at the picture, and it felt like the picture was staring back at me too!

The way he looked in that picture was how I wanted to remember my Daddy.

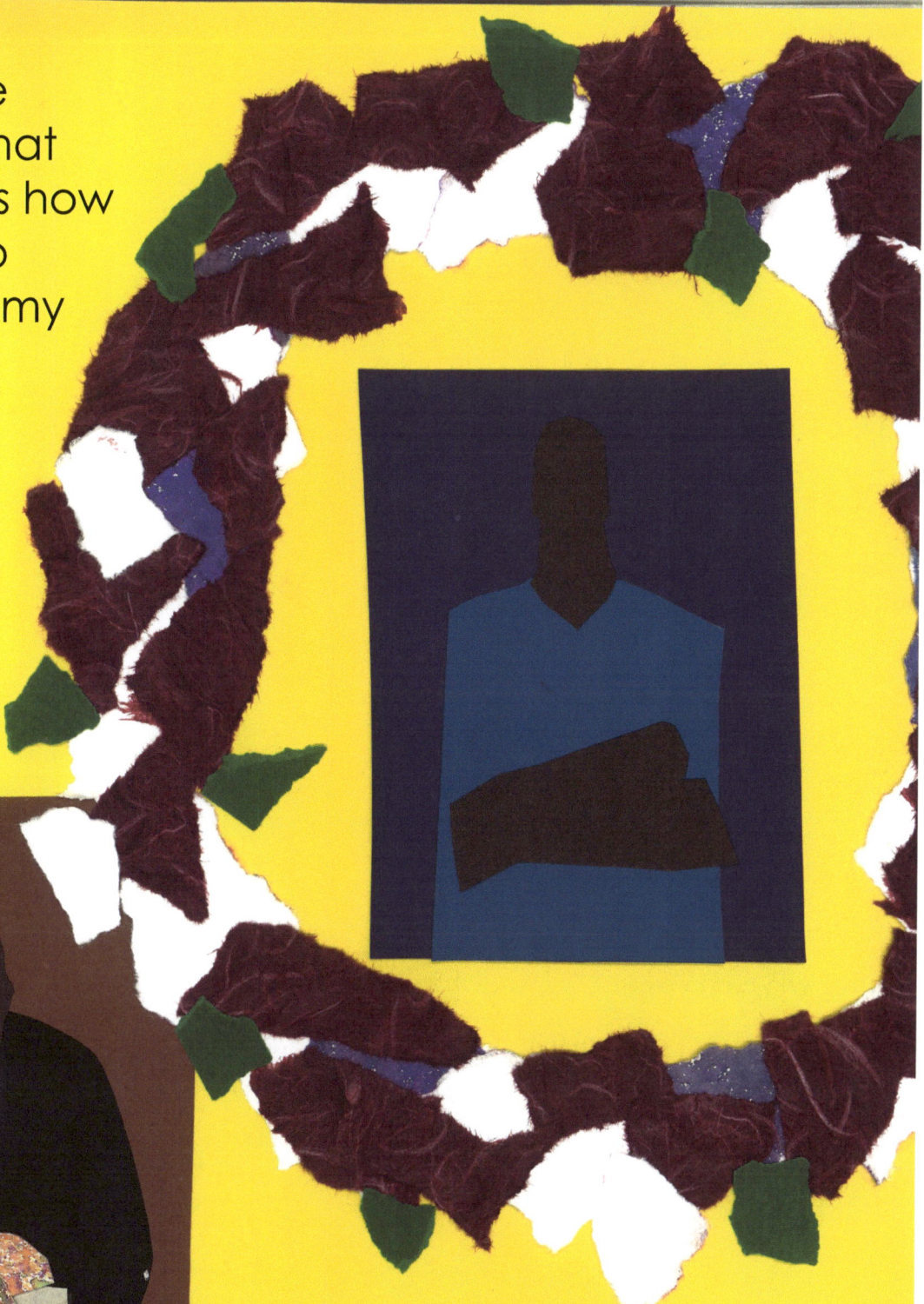

That's when I found out that even heroes have to leave someday.

I cried a lot that day. And the next day. I felt sad for a long time after that.

Then I got angry. I was angry that my Daddy had to get sick. Angry at him for going away. Angry at the doctors because they couldn't save him.

Why did *my Daddy* had to die? It was not fair. It made me upset.

But whenever I would get upset like that, I could talk to my Mama, Grandma, Granddaddy, my Auntie, or my Counselor. They would always listen to me and talk to me about it. Then they would hug me and make me feel better.

Right after Daddy died, I started going to see my counselor every Wednesday. I liked it because she had puppets to play with and I could paint pictures whenever I wanted.

My counselor talked with me about how I was feeling. She always made me feel like whatever I was feeling about my Daddy dying was o.k.

One day I was passing by a tree when I saw the body of a bird on the ground near the roots. It was a hatchling that had fallen out of the nest. Its wings were too weak to fly back to the treetop, and unable to get back to its mother, the bird had starved.

Seeing that bird's body reminded me that death is such a natural part of life that it's nothing to be afraid of.

Now when I look in the mirror, I see my Daddy living through me. I see his features in my face.

I keep all of the talents and abilities he passed on to me: All of my strength, all of my intelligence.

I remember what he taught me about how to treat other people.

These things will always be a part of me.

Resources for families near you:

About the Author

Artist and author Paul Singleton grew up in the town of Staunton, Virginia. A life-long artist, writer, and illustrator, Paul studied Art at Virginia Commonwealth University, where he obtained his Bachelor of Fine Arts degree in Art Education with a Minor in Psychology. Pursuing his interest in both Art (how we express ourselves) and Psychology (how we think and behave), Paul earned his Master of Arts degree in Art Therapy from New York University. When he's not making artwork, Paul helps other people tap into their imagination.